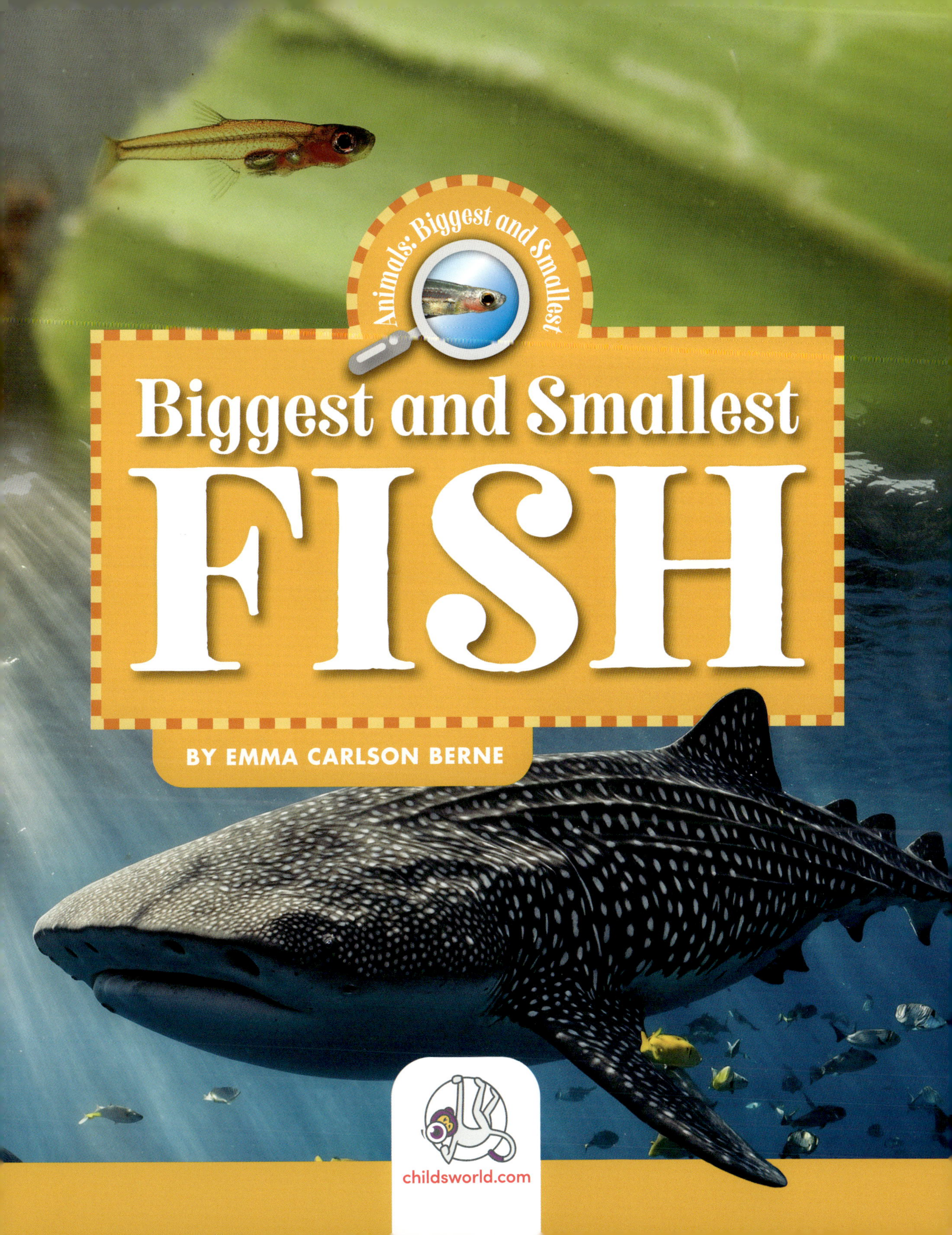
Animals: Biggest and Smallest
Biggest and Smallest
FISH
BY EMMA CARLSON BERNE
childsworld.com

Published by The Child's World®
800-599-READ • childsworld.com

Photography Credits
Cover: ©Ganjar Cahyadi/iNaturalist; ©Reehan Raza/Shutterstock; ©Liu S, Hui TH, Tan SL, Hong Y (2012) Chromosome Evolution and Genome Miniaturization in Minifish. PLoS ONE 7(5): e37305. https://doi.org/10.1371/journal.pone.0037305/PLoS ONE; ©mc_pongsatorn/Shutterstock; page 2: ©Liu S, Hui TH, Tan SL, Hong Y (2012) Chromosome Evolution and Genome Miniaturization in Minifish. PLoS ONE 7(5): e37305. https://doi.org/10.1371/journal.pone.0037305/PLoS ONE; page 5: ©mc_pongsatorn/Shutterstock; page 5: ©Justin Philbois/iNaturalist; page 6–7: ©Nick Utchin/Shutterstock; page 8–9: ©Reehan Raza/Shutterstock; page 11: ©Ganjar Cahyadi/iNaturalist; page 12–13: ©Paulo de Oliveira/NHPA/Avalon.red/Newscom; page 14–15: ©alvnzlfkr/Shutterstock; page 15: ©Jollanda/Shutterstock; page 15: ©Leontura/DigitalVision Vectors/Getty Images; page 16–17: ©Alexey Stiop/Shutterstock; page 18–19: ©Jason Edwards/The Image Bank/Getty Images; page 21: ©Animalgraphy/Shutterstock; page 22: ©Ann in the uk/Shutterstock; page 22: ©Lester Balajadia/Shutterstock.

ISBN Information
9781503875616 (Reinforced Library Binding)
9781503876149 (Portable Document Format)
9781503876767 (Online Multi-user eBook)
9781503877269 (Electronic Publication)

LCCN
2025938248

Printed in the United States of America

ABOUT THE AUTHOR

Emma Carlson Berne often writes about nature and animals, especially for young readers. She loves exploring the natural world in her free time as well. Emma lives in Cincinnati, Ohio, with her husband, three sons, one grumpy cat, and one friendly cat.

Table of Contents

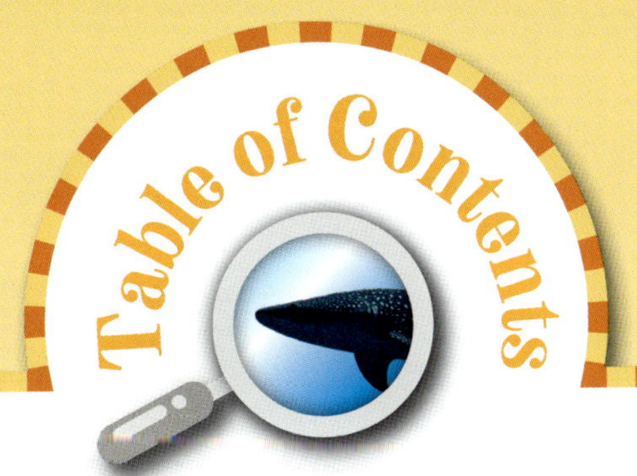

Big and Little

Animals' sizes help them live, hunt, and thrive in their environment. Big elephants and giraffes can travel easily through wide-open spaces such as grasslands. Small animals such as foxes can slip between trees in a forest. Over time, animals' sizes are affected by how much food is available. When animals can get more food, they **evolve** to be bigger. When animals have to compete for food, they might get smaller over time.

Off the coast of Australia lives a fish as long as a school bus. And in the swampy waters of southeast Asia is a fish no bigger than a pencil eraser. Big or small, these fish are perfectly **adapted** to their **habitats**.

Whale sharks are known as the gentle giants of the ocean.

The Indonesian superdwarf fish was discovered in 2006 by a scientist from Singapore.

Whale sharks live peacefully with many other kinds of fish.

Where Do Whale Sharks Live?

CHAPTER 2

Meet the Biggest!

The mighty whale shark is the biggest fish on Earth. This warmwater fish can weigh up to 20.6 tons, or 41,200 pounds (18,688 kilograms). That's as heavy as some fighter planes. Its tough spotted skin helps it blend in with patterns of light shining through the water.

The whale shark lives in warm oceans all over the planet. This giant fish doesn't grab **prey** with its teeth. Instead, it swims through clouds of small fish, **krill**, and **plankton**. It sucks them through a **filter** in its throat. Then, gulp! Down the food goes.

Whale sharks are often found close to the ocean's surface.

THE LITTLEST SHARK

Whale sharks are the biggest sharks, but what about the smallest? That prize goes to the dwarf lanternshark. This little fish can sit in the palm of a human hand. It swims in the Caribbean Sea along the coast of South America. But don't go searching for one next time you're out swimming. The dwarf lanternshark has only been spotted a handful of times.

Whale sharks sometimes have to dive deep into the ocean to get to the tiny animals they eat. It's cold down there! But scientists have learned that whale sharks' **organs** are surrounded by big chunks of muscle. This muscle helps keep their organs warm. The whale shark can stay warm for a long time. It can dive and hunt without getting cold. And it can get more food to eat!

Meet the Smallest!

Deep in the swampy waters of Sumatra lives one of the tiniest fish in the world. The *Paedocypris progenetica* (pee-do-SY-priss pro-jen-ET-ih-kuh) is about 0.4 inches (10.2 millimeters) long. The whole fish can fit on the tip of a person's finger. It is also known as the Indonesian superdwarf fish.

The Indonesian superdwarf fish's tiny size means that it uses very little oxygen to live. It is perfectly adapted to its home in the **peat** swamps where the water has low oxygen levels. These fish can hide from **predators** in rock cracks and under roots. They hunt and eat the tiny **zooplankton** that drift through the water.

Some people keep Indonesian superdwarf fish in their home aquariums.

Where Do Indonesian Superdwarf Fish Live?

Some of the world's smallest fish are only about as long as a human eyelash.

Many scientists believe the Indonesian superdwarf fish is the smallest fish in the world. But other fish are also in the running for this title. The *Photocorynus spiniceps* (foh-toh-KOR-ih-nus SPY-nuh-seps) male has been recorded at 0.2 inches (5.1 mm). It is also called the small anglerfish. It spends its life attached to the much bigger female. She's 1.8 inches (45.7 mm) long!

The stout floater fish lives in Australia's Great Barrier Reef. It has been measured at 0.3 inches (7.6 mm). But scientists argue that this fish is thinner than the Indonesian superdwarf fish and the male small anglerfish. Since it's a more slender fish, it also weighs less. The stout floater is the lightest fish in the world.

How They Compare

Most whale sharks are around 39 feet (11.9 meters) long. But they can grow up to 60 feet (18.3 m) long. The Indonesian superdwarf fish is as long as a pea! But these fish have some things in common.

Like all fish, both the whale shark and the Indonesian superdwarf fish have gills. These special organs make it possible for fish to breathe underwater. Water runs over the gills and goes into the fish's body. Then, the fish's body takes out the oxygen that is in the water.

MEASURING UP

An Indonesian superdwarf fish is about as long as a child's thumbnail. And about 13 kids could stretch out head-to-toe next to the largest known whale shark. That's really small—and really big!

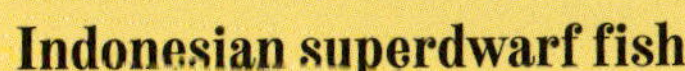

Indonesian superdwarf fish

Length: 0.4 inches (10.2 mm)

Weight: About 1 milligram

Average 10-year-old child

Height: 55 inches (1.4 m)

Weight: 70.5 pounds (32 kg)

Whale shark

Length: Up to 60 feet (18.3 m)

Weight: Up to 20.6 tons (18,688 kg)

FILTER FEEDERS

Some filter feeders, such as whale sharks, can suck water and fish in and let water flow out their gills. At other times, they might swim with their mouths open, letting water in without sucking. Other filter feeders, including baleen whales, have plates of stiff fibers inside their mouths. These let water flow out while trapping fish inside. Some **mollusks**, including clams, suck water in, then push it out in one blurp!

But even though both of these fish have gills, they don't have the same type. The Indonesian superdwarf fish has just one gill opening on each side of its body. It also has a bony plate over the gills that can open and close. The whale shark has five gills on each side. Its gills are open all the time with no protective plate.

Although both whale sharks and Indonesian superdwarf fish have gills, fins, and tails, their skeletons are very different. Whale sharks are part of a unique group of fish with skeletons made of cartilage. Human ears and noses contain this flexible, tough tissue. Cartilage is lighter than bone. This light skeleton helps sharks swim quickly through the water.

Like most other fish, Indonesian superdwarf fish have skeletons made of bones. This skeleton includes a spine, ribs, a jaw, and a skull. Bony fish also have a swim bladder. This air-filled organ helps the fish stay afloat in the water without using too much energy.

The pattern on a whale shark's skin helps it blend in with its surroundings.

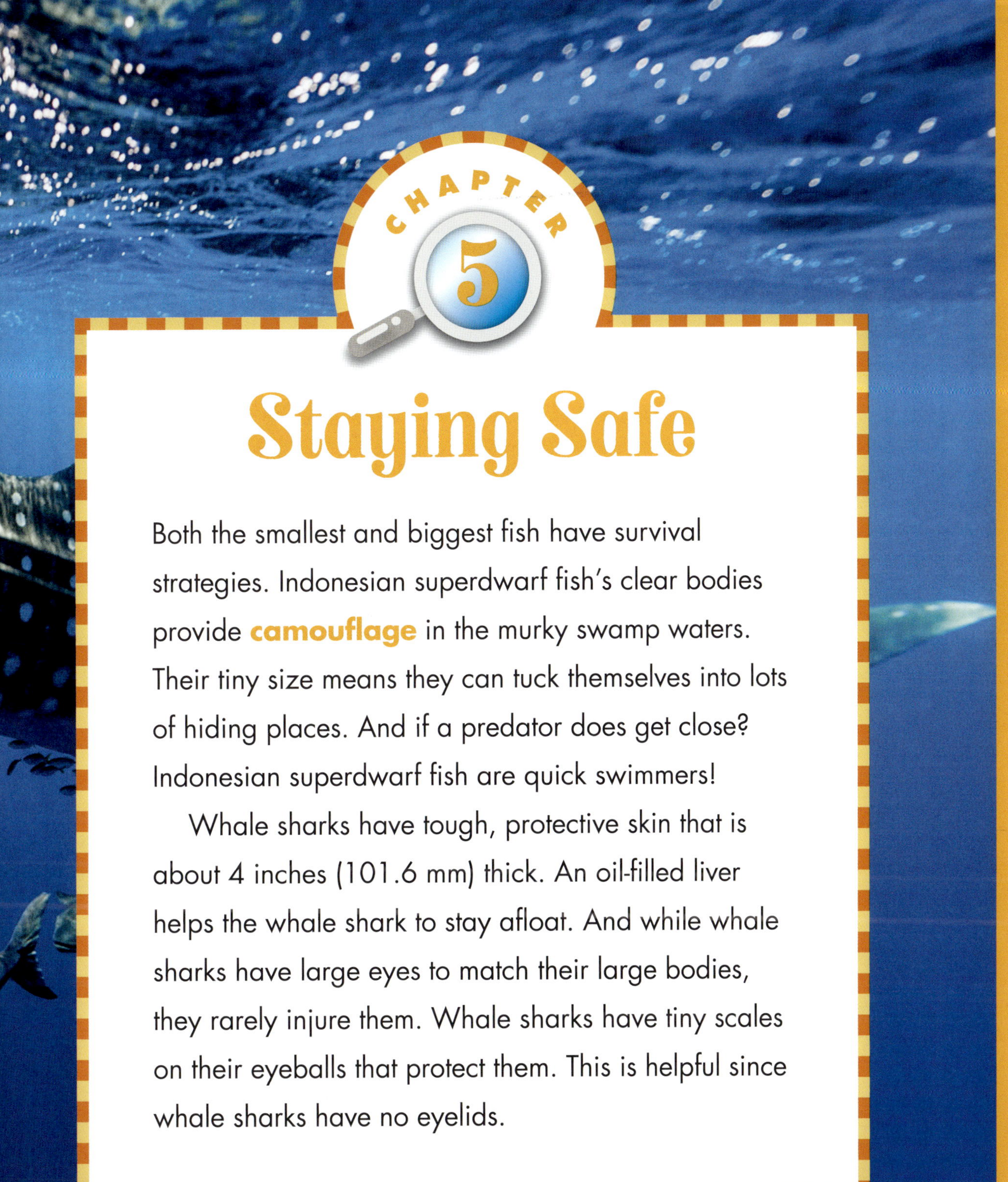

CHAPTER 5

Staying Safe

Both the smallest and biggest fish have survival strategies. Indonesian superdwarf fish's clear bodies provide **camouflage** in the murky swamp waters. Their tiny size means they can tuck themselves into lots of hiding places. And if a predator does get close? Indonesian superdwarf fish are quick swimmers!

Whale sharks have tough, protective skin that is about 4 inches (101.6 mm) thick. An oil-filled liver helps the whale shark to stay afloat. And while whale sharks have large eyes to match their large bodies, they rarely injure them. Whale sharks have tiny scales on their eyeballs that protect them. This is helpful since whale sharks have no eyelids.

A Better Future

Whale sharks and Indonesian superdwarf fish may have different sizes, diets, and skeletons, but they are similar in one important way. Both of these fish are under threat in their environment. The whale shark is at risk of dying out because of overfishing. Whale sharks are also easily struck by boat propellers. They get tangled in fishing lines and nets.

The ocean's waters are getting warmer, causing ice to melt and ocean levels to rise higher. These rising oceans threaten the Indonesian superdwarf fish's swampy, coastal habitat. Scientists are studying ways to protect the world's biggest and smallest fish so they can continue to be part of the ocean world for the future.

WONDER MORE

Wondering About New Information:

What is one new piece of information you learned by reading this book? Were you surprised by this information? Why or why not?

Wondering How It Matters:

Scientists are still finding new animals and investigating new discoveries. Why is it important to keep asking questions about the natural world?

Wondering Why:

Why might a fish grow larger or smaller over a long period of time?

Ways to Keep Wondering:

What questions do you still have about the biggest and smallest fish?

MAKE YOUR OWN TINY FISH

Supplies

- a flat, oval-shaped rock
- scissors
- glue
- thin, colored cardboard (Cut-up cereal or food boxes work well!)
- paint and a paintbrush

Using a few simple craft supplies, you can make your tiny fish. Then, display your creation in a special spot.

Directions

1. If your rock came from outside, scrub it in the sink and dry it well.
2. Using your scissors, cut out three small triangles from your colored cardboard. These will be the fins for your fish.
3. Place one triangle at the top of your rock and one at the bottom. These are your flippers. Place the third triangle at the end for the tail. Glue your triangles in place.
4. Get painting! Paint your fish with stripes, dots, or any other pattern. Don't forget a dot for the eye.
5. Let your fish dry and admire your work!

GLOSSARY

adapted (uh-DAP-tud) Animals that have adapted have changed to fit their environment.

camouflage (KA-muh-flazh) Camouflage helps animals disguise themselves to blend into their environment.

evolve (ee-VOLV) To evolve is to undergo change over time.

filter (FIL-tur) A filter is an object that water can pass through but which traps small objects.

habitat (HAB-uh-tat) A habitat is where an animal lives.

krill (KRIL) Krill are tiny shrimplike crustaceans.

mollusk (MOL-usk) A mollusk is an invertebrate with a soft body, often with an outer shell, that lives in wet or damp environments.

organs (OR-ganz) Organs are parts of the body that perform specific jobs, such as the heart and lungs.

peat (PEET) Peat is a dark brown soil-like material found in bogs and swamps.

plankton (PLANK-tun) Plankton are tiny floating plantlike organisms that float in water.

predator (PREH-duh-tur) A predator is an animal that hunts other animals for food.

prey (PRAY) Prey are animals that are hunted and eaten by other animals.

zooplankton (zoh-uh-PLANK-tun) Zooplankton are tiny floating animals that live in water.

FIND OUT MORE

In the Library

Brown, Kendra. *Small but Mighty: Why Earth's Tiny Creatures Matter.* Toronto, Ontario, CAN: Owlkids Books, 2021.

Kurtz, Kevin. *Fish for Kids: A Junior Scientist's Guide to Diverse Habitats, Colorful Species, and Life Underwater.* Rockridge Press, Emeryville, CA, 2021.

Regan, Lisa, and Patrick Corrigan. *How Big?: Animals.* London, UK: Arcturus, 2024.

On the Web

Visit our website for links about the biggest and smallest fish:
childsworld.com/links

Note to Parents, Caregivers, Teachers, and Librarians: We routinely verify our web links to make sure they are safe and active sites. So encourage your readers to check them out!

INDEX